HENRY COHEN

The Life of a
Frontier Rabbi

ḤENRY COḤEN

The Life of a
Frontier Rabbi

By
Jimmy Kessler

EAKIN PRESS ★ Austin, Texas

Contents

iii

Rabbi Henry Cohen
—Courtesy Temple B'Nai Israel, Galveston

Preface:
A Brief Look at a Long Life

Being a pioneer, on the frontier as well as in his ideas, was not unique in the life of Rabbi Henry Cohen. He started this path as a boy in the poor areas of London, giving out, along with his childhood friend Israel Zangwill, charity funds for Lord Moses Montifiore. Cohen's experiences would eventually come to include his years in Africa, his service in Kingston, Jamaica, and finally his sixty-two years in Galveston, Texas, from 1888 to 1950.

Rabbi Cohen's life took him to many parts of the world, but his presence in those frontier communities in frontier times influenced his ideas, his activities, and his teachings as much as his worldly travels did. As a result, Dr. Cohen's life served as a major influence on areas of the Jewish and non-Jewish experience in the Southwest. And his many years of service and his prominence carried his influence to a national level.

As the Rabbi of Temple B'nai Israel for sixty-two years, Cohen had an incredible view from which to see and comment upon world history. It is clear that Dr. Cohen wanted to be intimately involved with not only the Galveston Island community but with the greater community as well. And all of this was done from a frontier vantage point.

Of all the roles Dr. Cohen filled, it was that of facilitator which was most important. A facilitator was one who brought together all the components of a desired action so that the desired results were achieved. In the case of Rabbi Cohen, it was through facilitating that those new on the frontier, whether new immigrants or native transplants, were able to fit into American society without losing ties to their heritage.

Rabbi Cohen's guide for his work was the passage from the Prophet Micah (6:8): "It has been told you, O man, what is good and what the Lord requires of you; to do justly, to love mercy and to walk humbly with your God." Dr. Cohen did so his entire life. So much occurred during his time in the pulpit that it is nearly impossible to report on all of his life. But a day in the life of Rabbi Cohen, as follows, will provide a clear picture of the man and his work.

1/Galveston's Dr. Cohen

Rabbi Henry Cohen looked at his cuff, slipped on his frock coat about 8:00 A.M., just as he had done for the past fifty-seven years on Galveston Island, and thought about his appointments for this tenth day of December, 1945, as well as the coming festival of Chanukah. White tie neatly bowed, Dexter shoes well worn, small cigars in his pocket, the Rabbi set off on his daily rounds for this Monday.

Though the lead article in the *Galveston Daily News*, the oldest newspaper in Texas, spoke of Gen. George Patton, Jr.'s serious injury in an automobile accident in Germany, it was the article on Adolf Hitler ordering Jews to be used in spy work in America which troubled the Rabbi. Cohen had seen numerous examples of anti-Semitism in his eighty-two years of life, as well as other forms of hatred. This planted lie by World War II German prisoners was another example of the Nazis' attempt to destroy America. It was just another example of how, if someone wanted to mislead people to do bad things, all they had to do was create a lie so big and so silly that everyone believed it. Hitler had said that the Jews were the cause of all of Germany's problems, including the presence of rats in the country. People believed him, and the Holocaust was the result.

Cohen remembered that just such a lie was spread years before, when the *Merchant of Venice*, a play by the English author William Shakespeare, was taught in the Galveston high schools. One of the teachers was saying that all Jews were like the character Shylock, who demanded payment of debts no matter how it hurt the family or person who owed it. As someone born and raised in England where the poor, like himself, were kept in special areas and never allowed to make a better life, Cohen knew that Shakespeare never knew any Jews and based his description of Shylock on old anti-Semitic attitudes. The Rabbi quickly paid a visit to the Superintendent of schools and arranged for some other plays of Shakespeare to be taught instead.

Rabbi Cohen headed for his car, which was driven by a chauffeur. The Rabbi drove

2

himself when cars first came to Galveston. However, it seemed that whenever he got behind the wheel of his car, his mind would wander to whom he was to visit next and to where he was going, or his eyes would glance down at his cuff to see his next scheduled stop. As a result, his driving was a bit irregular. After a number of years of this familiar lovable road danger, the community, and especially the police chief, convinced the Rabbi to get a driver. The chief was not worried about wrecks, but rather that some new officer would stop the Rabbi and arrest him, not knowing who he was.

For fifty-seven years, the five-foot-one-inch Rabbi had ridden his bike down these well-known streets he was now crossing in his car. Riding his bike with his coattails flying in the breeze, he had been able to accomplish most of his tasks in short time. Now, with a car, he seemed to get around in an even shorter period of time. But even with the chauffeur he acquired, there weren't enough hours in a day to do everything. At least the road danger was removed.

During his time as Rabbi of Temple B'nai Israel, Henry Cohen was offered the presidency of the Hebrew Union College, the Rabbinical school for Reform Rabbis. In addition, he received several honorary doctorate degrees over his lifetime. It became standard for people to refer to him as Dr. Cohen. The term became so commonly used that newcomers to the University of Texas Medical Branch at Galveston (UTMB) generally assumed that when others referred to Dr. Cohen, they meant a very famous physician on staff, particularly from the way they spoke of him.

For as long as anyone could remember, Rabbi Cohen always wore Dexter shoes and white bow ties and smoked cigars. Yet, of all his trademarks, the most well known were his shirt cuffs. He wore shirts which had no cuffs attached; that is, in addition to putting on a shirt, he also had to put cuffs on at the end of each sleeve. Upon those cuffs the Rabbi wrote notes and kept his daily appointment list. As a result, he regularly either wrote on them or read from them; hence, the driving problem.

As the Rabbi settled into his car, he waved at Mollie. They had been married for fifty-six years and shared many good and bad times. With two children and two grandchildren, they had many memories. Harry, their son, followed a career in journalism and Henry, Harry's son, was on his way to becoming a Rabbi. The Cohens' daughter Ruth died too young, but David, her son, would receive a doctorate and teach.

Henry smiled as he recalled the newspaper article of over one-half century before which announced his marriage to Mollie. "A fatal matrimonial malady befalls all clergy who arrive at Temple B'nai Israel as a bachelor," or

4

something like that, was how the newspaper article began. It was true. Just as Rabbi Silverman, who preceded Cohen as Rabbi of B'nai Israel, married a Galveston girl, so did Henry.

Mollie was clearly his "other half." She ran a wonderful home, entertaining their guests and always ready for the people Henry brought home for dinner without telling her. And she managed a good deal of the family finances. Mollie even kept his suits clean of cigar ash, at least as best she could.

Over their half-century together, Henry had invaded his house with so many hundreds of books that a third-floor library had to be built. The Cohens lived at 1920 Broadway, in a home referred to as the rabbinage, provided by Temple B'nai Israel, through the generosity of the Kempner family. It was the only minister's home in the world in which a Rabbi lived that was formally called the rabbinage.

As the Rabbi straightened his coat, he reflected on his invention from years before. Just as his father had invented and patented a switch for the gas lamp in England, so, too, did the good Rabbi try his luck. His contribution was a frock coat like most, but with one addition. Near the middle button, on the left-hand side, sewn into the lining, was a small pocket. Into this pocket, the owner was to place calling cards. After shaking hands with a new acquaintance, the person could easily reach into that slit and readily present a card to the new comrade.

Rabbi Cohen's parents were of very limited means. David had worked as a tinsmith and Josephine stayed busy with seven children. Born in 1863, Rabbi Cohen began his early education at Jews' Hospital, a school whose students usually went on to the University of London. Henry had a photographic memory and an ability with other languages, so he finished his studies at the hospital at the age of fifteen. Instead of going on to a university, he went to work at the Board of Guardians, assisting with Jews in need and attending night classes at Jews' College.

At the age of eighteen, Henry interrupted his studies to travel with his older brother, Mark, to Cape Town in Africa. Though Mark was seven years older, he and Henry maintained a correspondence long after they each had settled into lives in different countries. Of all the events of their trip, the Rabbi liked to tell the story of his close call with the Zulus.

Henry stayed in Africa and found himself in the town of Robertson, where he got a temporary job in a general store operated by the Steinmans. One morning in February 1883, Henry found himself humming the words to the *Pirates of Penzance* by Gilbert and Sullivan while he was working in the store.

Suddenly, a bugle rang out and Mr. Steinman hurriedly arrived, giving Henry a rifle and posting him near the store. The Rabbi only remembered singing the words of *Pirates*, over and over, when suddenly the gun was wrenched out of his hands by a Zulu Kaffir and the butt of it smashed over his head. He fell unconscious to the ground. Though he recovered, his family was sent a telegram by the British War Office, saying that Henry was killed.

Upon returning to England, Henry went back to Jews' College and continued his preparation for a career in the Jewish community. He became trained as a *shochet* and *mohel*, and in 1884 set off for the British West Indies. For one year he served the Amalgamated Congregation of Israelites.

All his life Cohen had heard about Jamaica rum. At a dinner one night at the home of Hyam Barrow, president of the congregation, Henry asked to taste the rum. Mr. Barrow poured a small glassful of the dark liquid for the Rabbi to enjoy. Cohen said a blessing, downed the rum in one gulp, and then collapsed on the nearby couch. He slept twenty-four hours. The Rabbi found out that it not only tasted good, but was quite potent too.

Rabbi Cohen's next move took him to Woodville, Mississippi, and his first formal affiliation with the Reform Jewish movement. Reform Judaism in America was started on its road by many Rabbis in the mid-1800s, but the most well known was Rabbi Isaac Mayer Wise. He established the Union of American Hebrew Congregations to be an affiliation of Reform synagogues, the Hebrew Union College to train and ordain Rabbis devoted to Reform, and a professional organization of Reform Rabbis called the Central Conference of American Rabbis. Galveston, Texas, and Temple B'nai Israel were Cohen's next stop and his last stop. He arrived in 1888, and there he remained for sixty-two years.

As the car traveled down the street, Dr. Cohen remembered that Chanukah was soon to take place. This Jewish festival always seemed a bit different. It was the celebration of the first recorded military battle where people fought for freedom of religion. The Jewish people fought the Hasmoneans, who were ruling Israel about 150 B.C.E., and who had taken over the Temple in Jerusalem.

The history of the events in Jerusalem in the days of Chanukah teaches that a Jew named Judah Maccabee called together a group of farmers, and they attacked the Hasmoneans. They were successful in driving them out of the Temple. The goal of the Hasmoneans was to keep the Jews from worshiping God the way they wanted to. So, they outlawed the circumcision of Jewish boys on the eighth day of their life, they put an eagle in the Temple where the Jews prayed, and they wanted to offer sacrifices to their gods in the Temple. As a result, the Jewish people rebelled. After all, one of the most important messages in the Bible is the freedom people should have to worship as they want.

Rabbi Cohen remembered with a smile the numerous Chanukah celebrations in his home, for this was a home and family holiday. A special candle holder was used, a *chanukiyah*, which holds nine candles. The candles represented the legend which grew up around the military battle.

In the Temple of King Solomon, a light made from burning oil was always kept burning over the altar. It was called the eternal light and was a symbol that the Lord was always present in the Temple. When the Selucids took over, they destroyed all of the oil and put out the burning light. After the Jews had retaken the Temple, they wanted to relight the eternal flame. They found there was only one day's worth of oil. That oil, however, lasted eight days, which was the time it took them to make new oil. In celebration of the miracle, an additional candle is lit each day during Chanukah until all eight are burning. The ninth is used to light the other eight.

Cohen reflected on those candles, the *latkes*, the jelly-filled doughnuts, the gifts and candy which were part of the festival. Each child received multiple gifts on each of the eight nights. Not a bad eight days for a kid growing up, he thought.

Well, Chanukah was coming and the

morning was cool and crisp, as were many Texas December mornings, and the Rabbi had a full day ahead. So with notes on his cuff, white bow tie neatly made, and several cigars in his pocket, the Rabbi was off and about.

2/Hatred

Still riding in his car, Cohen was drawn from his thoughts of Chanukah by the image of Jim Kirwin in the window of St. Mary's Infirmary. The Catholic Monsignor and the Rabbi had met many years before.

When Cohen was new to Galveston, Kirwin, then a priest, was assigned to St. Mary's Infirmary. Over the decades, they looked an odd couple, Cohen being slightly over five feet tall and Kirwin being over six feet. But together they sought to make Galveston a better place to live. They fought the Ku Klux Klan, illegal gambling, and prostitution on the Island. They were the best of friends.

Some of the best times Cohen spent with Kirwin were the Shabbat dinners at the

Rabbi's home. The Jewish Shabbat, the Hebrew word for "Sabbath," began at sundown on Friday and ended at sundown on Saturday. It was the Jewish tradition to calculate days from sundown because the Bible says, "It was evening, it was morning, day one."

Though the Rabbi had to conduct services on Friday night and Saturday morning, he never missed the enjoyment of the family and friends gathered at his dinner table following Friday night services. He always began his services at 6:00 P.M. and was at his dinner table by 7:00.

Part of the Sabbath rituals he enjoyed sharing with friends, like Msgr. Kirwin, were the candles which were lit before dinner, the cup of wine which was sipped, and the bread which was blessed and then eaten. These blessings gave thanks for many gifts, particularly the lights of the sun and moon, the sweetness of the many things which could be grown, such as grapes for the wine, and the wheat for flour and bread.

The Sabbath dinner table was also a time to catch up on what was going on in everyone's life and to discuss many topics. Since Rabbi Cohen regularly invited someone to dinner, there were new topics to be discussed. It was always a lively dinner table and a joyous Shabbat.

Although times such as the Sabbath were festive and joyous, the Rabbi's work centered on very serious matters. For more than fifty-two years, Dr. Cohen was involved with many events which demonstrated how badly some people treated others just because they had a different religion, or looked different, or came from a different place. As a Rabbi, he was first involved with fighting those who would do harm to the Jewish people. In his lifetime, he saw a great deal of anti-Semitism, in Galveston, in Texas, in the United States, and in the world. Where he could, he fought against it by his writings and his actions.

The Rabbi knew that not all anti-Semitism was open and public; some was almost silent and yet very, very dangerous. He remembered one incident that reminded him of how even the nicest people can pass on the worst views of the Jewish people.

One of the unique programs that Rabbi Cohen established was the Temple Forum. This was a public lecture series, held at Temple B'nai Israel, which was open and free to the entire community. The speakers were not only interesting people who lived in Galveston but also those who were visiting the Island. It was a chance for the entire community to hear other opinions and ideas, and to ease some of the prejudices.

At one such gathering, the speaker was a Baptist minister who had known Dr. Cohen for many years. During his lecture, the minister said that Jews were not going to heaven as they were cursed. A hush passed over the mixed audience. A small-framed, elderly woman stood up and asked if, after all that Rabbi Cohen had done, he was included in that group. When the minister said that, yes, Rabbi Cohen was going to hell, the lady rapped her walking cane on the wooden floor and told him that she would rather go to hell with Henry Cohen than to heaven with him. She turned and walked out.

Rabbi Cohen smiled as he recalled the story. It always reminded him of Passover. Passover is the major Jewish festival observed in the spring which celebrates the exodus from Egypt of the Jews. The book of Exodus, in the Bible, records the story of the miracles which God performed to free the Jewish people from slavery to Pharaoh and from the laws which kept them from praying to God the way they wanted. During this seven-day celebration, the Jews don't eat bread. It is a way of remembering that the slaves weren't free to eat what they wanted nor were they given time to prepare food they wanted. A cracker-like food called *matzah* is eaten to remind Jews of this story.

As the Rabbi remembered the story of Passover, he also remembered that Jews are taught not to cheer at the death of their enemies. When the ten plagues are recalled at the Passover *seder*, each person must remove a drop of wine from their cup, so that they decrease their enjoyment. It always impressed Cohen that his tradition never allowed him to be happy at other people's sadness, even if they were his foe.

Perhaps the story of the minister reminded him of Passover because it was a celebration of freedom. Not just freedom from slavery, but from the bondage of not being able to pray. Freedom of religion has always been a major concern of the Jewish people and something for which Cohen always fought. It was also understood by him that the founding fathers of America saw themselves as the descendants of the Jews historically because they were escaping the slavery of Europe. Benjamin Franklin went so far as to suggest that the great seal of the United States should be an image of the Jewish people crossing the Red Sea.

Cohen, however, did not stop with those who attacked the Jewish people. He also fought against all injustice, particularly in Galveston and Texas. Galveston, as a port city, was a place of both legal and illegal activities. Before the 1900 hurricane, the city was the major business center in Texas. Cotton was a large part of the goods shipped out of Galveston to Europe, where it was made into cloth and then shipped back to the United States. As a result, many things entered the country through Galveston, and people arrived there seeking a new home and a new life.

Galveston, like other cities on the edge of

the frontier of a growing America, was home to those who wanted to establish honest living conditions with good educational programs, fine cultural activities, and a safe community in which to raise a family. But Galveston businesses were willing to welcome even the rougher elements as long as they spent money. A struggle developed between the two attitudes, and many times the same people supported both sides. At the same time that the famous Galveston Opera House was built in 1894, gambling was going on illegally.

The Ku Klux Klan was revived in the United States in 1915. The Klan came into existence after the Civil War. It was organized by some people who were unhappy with the outcome of the American Civil War. They wanted to put fear into the minds of the freed slaves and to try to make people vote for candidates supported by the Klan.

After World War I, the Ku Klux Klan became more active in the United States, as did other groups and individuals who hated Jews, African Americans, Hispanics, and Catholics. In the 1920s the Klan found its way into Texas politics. Every effort to enter Galveston failed, including an attempt to march down Market Street which was stopped by Father Kirwin. When the parade was announced, the priest threatened to give the paraders an ample dose of tear gas from St. Mary's Infirmary.

At another time when the Klan decided to hold a rally and cross burning on Galveston Island, the Rabbi and the Catholic priest decided it wouldn't happen. In those days, the only bridge to the Island was a railroad bridge with narrow car lanes. The night of the scheduled rally, Cohen and Kirwin were driven in a truck to the middle of the bridge, where the truck was turned sideways to block the Klan parade of cars from entering the Island. The Klan could do nothing but turn around. Even though there were many more Klan members and most had guns, they were afraid to harm the two ministers. Of course, it didn't hurt that behind the Rabbi and the Priest were a large number of sheriff's deputies armed with even more guns than the Klan had. When the Klan asked why they were being stopped, the sheriff responded that they weren't there to stop the Klan from meeting — they were just there to help Rabbi Cohen and Father Kirwin with their car trouble.

The Klan was not the only source of concern for the Jewish community. Cohen also responded to those who sought to attack the Jewish community directly. The American Mission to the Jews wanted to teach the Jews that their religion wasn't good and that all the Jews ought to convert to Christianity. They even wrote Dr. Cohen for a list of the Jews whom they could contact. Obviously, Rabbi Cohen didn't answer them. He believed that everyone had a right to worship the way he or she wanted to and that no one should be told what to believe.

Rabbi Cohen also tried to change the attitudes of individuals in Galveston. The local newspaper, the *Galveston News,* was run by Major Lowe. It seemed to Cohen that every time something happened to a member of the Jewish community, the Major labeled the person as being a Hebrew. This practice bothered the Rabbi greatly, as he never saw Lowe mention any other person's religion.

One day, Cohen read that a fire had occurred, but the religion of the owner was not in the newspaper article. The Rabbi immediately went down to the newspaper and walked in on Major Lowe. When he asked Lowe the man's religion, the Major wanted to know what difference it made. Cohen explained that it was very funny that whenever a bad thing happened involving one of the Jews in town, Lowe pointed out the person's religion. So, the Rabbi wanted to know why the religion of this man was not reported in the newspaper story. Major Lowe thought a moment about what he had done and then promised the Rabbi that it would never happen again. And it didn't.

Then there was the time that Rabbi Cohen went to visit two men in jail, Lipsky and Feder, both Jewish. They had been arrested for minor theft. The men asked the Rabbi for money by which to get out of Galveston. The Rabbi knew that they had been arrested previously, trying to get money from anyone and using any excuse. When Cohen told them that he would give them no money, but that they should get out of town, they threatened him.

Some days later, while Cohen was on the porch with his kids, the two criminals appeared at his home. One demanded money in a threatening way. The Rabbi tricked one of them to look at the floor, and when the man did, Cohen gave him a right to the chin and knocked him off the second-level porch. The man's companion ran away. Though the Rabbi didn't want his children, Ruth and Harry, to see the event, he helped them understand that sometimes a person has to do such things.

The Rabbi smiled as he continued his trip downtown in the car, reflecting upon those times of difficulty in the past. His attention was brought back from his daydreaming to issues of more immediate concern when the car pulled up to the offices of the U.S. National Bank. The notes on his cuff reminded him of the phone call he was to make to the governor late that afternoon and the lunch appointment he had with the dean of the medical school. In the meantime, he would meet with Mr. Kempner about the needs of the new immigrants who would be coming to America's shores now that World War II was over.

It would be another full day for Dr. Henry Cohen, Rabbi.

3/Immigrants

As Rabbi Cohen rode up in the elevator to the offices of H. Kempner Co. for his 10:30 A.M. appointment, he began to think about the project of settling new immigrants to the United States from other parts of the war-torn world. This was not the first time that Cohen had been involved with those who sought to find a better way of life.

As a youngster in London, Cohen remembered the days he spent delivering money and food to those in need in the poor sections of the city. He knew how poverty could hurt because it destroyed hope and the person's feeling of self-worth. Poverty would cause even more problems for those who were strangers in a new land.

Hope is a major part of Jewish tradition, not only for the Jewish people, but for individual Jews as well. Two of the most well-known Jewish holy days deal with that theme. Rosh Hashanah, the Jewish religious new year, which usually occurs in September, speaks of the possibilities for new and good things in the new year. A trumpet made of a ram's horn, called a *shofar*, is sounded on this holy day to remind people of how special it is.

Ten days later, the holy day Yom Kippur, the Jewish day of atonement, gives Jews a special day to think about their lives and how they behave. The purpose of this holy day is to encourage the people to live their lives more in keeping with the highest traditions of Judaism. To help Jews concentrate on this festival, they are not permitted to eat or drink on this day and they spend it in the synagogue.

One of the greatest freedoms America granted the Jewish immigrants, as well as all others, was freedom of religion. The government did not force a religion on the people, and people were allowed to pray as they wanted. Having seen other parts of the world where such freedom did not exist, Dr. Cohen understood how important that freedom was.

Immigration to the United States came in different waves of people. Among the Jewish people, there were three major waves. The first was from the 1700s through the mid-1800s.

Most of those people came from Spain, North Africa, and the Scandinavian countries. The second wave of Jewish immigrants began in the mid-1800s and ran through the early 1900s, and most of them came from the Germanic countries. The third major wave began in the late 1800s and has lasted through today. Those in the third wave have mostly come from eastern European countries, particularly Russia.

At one time in the history of the United States, Galveston was the second largest port of entry for immigrants. There was a great need for help in moving these newcomers on to homes and jobs. Some remained on the Island or in the area, while others moved on to other cities and states. Although Henry Cohen was one of those who came to these shores through another port of entry, he, too, was an immigrant and became a citizen on October 12, 1896.

Even though the United States was considered a wonderful place in which to live, many, including Jews, desired to remain in the old countries. In the late 1800s this feeling began to end because of a terrible injustice in France, which affected many other countries. A Jewish captain in the French army named Alfred Dreyfus was accused of giving military secrets to the Germans. It took many years for Dreyfus to be cleared, but during that time a major wave of anti-Semitism arose. Jews found it very difficult to live in their homelands as they all were labeled as traitors.

In Russia, the Jews had been the property of the landowner on whose land they lived. No matter where they moved, the same laws applied. Since the Jews had no rights, they could ask for no help from anyone when trouble arose. In the late 1800s a number of pogroms, organized attacks on helpless people, were launched against the Jews of Russia. One of the worst was in Kishineff. Numerous Jews were killed and others were driven from their homes by the Black Hundred, a group supported by the Czar. The Czar took the people's minds off the hard times by attacking the Jews. A past president of Rabbi Cohen's congregation, Leo N. Levi, convinced President Theodore Roosevelt and Secretary of State John Hay to protest to Czar Nicholas the Second about the massacres. It did no good. The pogroms continued.

Jews began to make their way to the United States, along with many others, who wanted to escape prejudice in Europe. One of the most important people in this country who recognized the need for doing something for these immigrants was Jacob Schiff, head of the banking firm of Kuhn, Loeb in New York. He understood the need to find a welcoming home for those seeking a new life.

At the same time Schiff was thinking about the needs of European Jews in the United States, so was Israel Zangwill in

London. This childhood friend of Henry Cohen knew that the Jews had to have a place to live where they could be free to practice Judaism and not be persecuted because of who they were. Soon Schiff and Zangwill joined forces, along with Morris Waldman, a Rabbi and social worker, and Henry Cohen, to operate a program that was to be called the Galveston Plan.

The arrangements were for Zangwill to obtain the names of those who might want to immigrate to the United States and send that information to Waldman. In turn, Waldman would find communities where the new residents could live and obtain jobs. Jacob Schiff provided the funds, Zangwill made all the travel arrangements, and Cohen met the immigrants in Galveston. The plan called for using Galveston because New York was overcrowded, and it seemed better to spread the immigration around the country.

The Jewish Immigrants' Information Bureau, the actual name of the Galveston Plan, was able to place 10,000 new immigrants in its seven years of operation beginning in 1907. The first immigrant ship to arrive in Galveston was the *Cassel* out of Hamburg, delivering sixty Jews from Russia. The mayor of Galveston, Mr. Landes, and Rabbi Cohen were there to greet the new arrivals. After their welcome, they started on their way to a new life.

In the first few years of the 1900s, many

people in the United States found it difficult to get jobs. Most of the lower paying jobs were being taken by new immigrants. As a result, public sentiment began to change. Immigrants were not as welcomed as they had been. In response to this new feeling, regulations were issued by the U.S. government that made it harder to enter the country and easier for the immigration officials to deport new arrivals.

In one case, Rabbi Cohen was informed that a recent immigrant, a boilermaker from Russia, was to be sent back because he arrived as a stowaway. The trouble was that if he returned to Russia, he would be shot by a firing squad. Rabbi Cohen went to appeal to the local immigration agent to arrange for permission for the man to remain in the United States. The agent refused; the man had to return. The Rabbi could not stand by and allow this to happen, so the next day he borrowed $100 and set off on a train for Washington, D.C. Cohen went to the Department of Labor, but they saw it as a clear case of illegal entry. The man had to return no matter what would happen in Russia, they said.

Dr. Cohen refused to abide by the ruling. He went immediately to his congressman's office, where it was arranged for him to see President William Howard Taft. The president was very friendly and listened to the story, but explained that there was nothing he could do. As the Rabbi slowly rose to leave, the president commented on how special it was for the Rabbi to come on behalf of another Jew. The Rabbi immediately told the president that the man was a Greek Catholic and not Jewish. President Taft was amazed that the Rabbi had traveled all that distance for a stranger who wasn't even Jewish. As a result, the president sent a telegram to Galveston ordering the agent not to deport the man and to turn him over to Rabbi Cohen.

Among the many immigrants who were able to remain in this country was the young Clara Reinhardt. She decided to remain in Galveston and earned her living cleaning houses and making delicious noodles. One day, when she was working at Rabbi Cohen's, he found her crying in the kitchen. When asked to explain, she told him that her brother was in Europe and she didn't have the money to bring him over to the United States. Dr. Cohen immediately raised the funds for his travel and gave the money to Clara, who arranged for his passage.

On the appointed day, Clara and the Rabbi went to the port to meet the ship which was carrying Clara's brother. As soon as they saw each other, the two met in an embrace and kiss which hardly looked like that of a brother and sister. After some minutes of kissing, Clara and Fred joined Rabbi Cohen. When the Rabbi asked about the brother, Clara broke into tears, admitting that she had lied. Fred was not Fred

Reinhardt, her brother, but Fred Nussenblatt, her fiancé. She was afraid that if she had told the truth, no one would have given her any help to bring her fiancé to Galveston. They married, remained in Galveston, and became active members of the Jewish community.

In addition to his activities with the Galveston Plan, the Rabbi was an early writer of Texas history and particularly Texas Jewish history. He interviewed family members of major figures in Texas history and sometimes the people themselves. He did research on the history of Jews in Texas through the Washington offices of the Departments of Agriculture, Insurance, Statistics and History. In 1936, Cohen organized and authored a book on the history of the Jews in Texas for the Texas Centennial celebration.

In this, his last decade as the Rabbi of B'nai Israel, Cohen would again be involved in helping immigrants, especially Jews, find new homes in America. As he rode in the elevator to the offices of I.H. Kempner, a prominent member of the Jewish and Galveston community, Cohen knew that these arrivals would be survivors of Hitler's attempt to kill every Jew in Europe. The Nazis of Germany, under the leadership of Adolf Hitler, had organized the final solution by which Europe would be rid of all its Jews — over six million people. This Holocaust, carried out by the

Nazis during World War II, destroyed over half the Jewish population in the world.

Cohen and the Jewish community of Galveston stood ready to help those who had survived.

4/No Catholic Arthritis, or Jewish Mumps

After securing the assistance of I. H. Kempner in the settlement of new immigrants, Cohen left the U.S. National Bank building for the University of Texas Medical School.

Founded in 1890, the medical school in Galveston was not only the oldest such school in Texas, but the oldest west of the Mississippi. The Rabbi was the first Jewish chaplain to the school and its hospital. Over the past half-century, the Rabbi had been a regular figure on campus.

Today, as he headed out to the east end of the Island to have lunch with the dean of the medical school, he recalled the speech he had given at the Galveston Rotary Club. In it he had noted that there was no Episcopalian scarlet fever, no Catholic arthritis, and no Jewish mumps. To Cohen, anyone who was sick was deserving of attention. It was his practice to go up and down the halls, visiting with anyone he knew or who needed help. Moreover, it was not uncommon for the Rabbi to be called out to the hospitals to visit people who were not Jewish but who believed his prayers could help them get better.

The Rabbi also smiled at less serious visits to the medical school. There was the time he burst into the surgery suite, where the chairman of the department, Dr. Singleton, was performing an operation and was being assisted by a young Jewish intern. Protected only by a surgical mask he held to his face and a surgical gown only slightly pulled over his arms, the Rabbi stood wagging his finger at the intern, telling her that he had not seen her at services in weeks and he wanted to see her that coming Sabbath. As he left he heard Dr. Singleton command the intern that she had better be at services at the Temple that night if she wanted to come back to school the following week. After all, he didn't want Rabbi Cohen calling on him.

Dr. Cohen also recalled the time that he explained Jewish festivals to several visitors to the medical school. Particularly, he remembered their interest in Sukkot and Shavuot. Both of these are called pilgrimage holidays established in the Bible.

Sukkot is the holiday which follows Yom

Kippur and celebrates the fall agricultural harvest. It also was the time that Jews were to come to the Temple in Jerusalem. Cohen used to explain that the modern celebration of the seven-day festival included building booths, *sukkot,* of palm leaves where some people eat all their meals during the holiday.

Fifty days after Passover, the other major pilgrimage festival, called Shavuot, is celebrated. The holiday, which means "weeks" and represents the seven weeks between the exodus from Egypt and the giving of the Torah on Mt. Sinai, celebrates the giving of the Torah. Many congregations, including B'nai Israel of Galveston, celebrate this holiday by holding the graduation of religious school students in a confirmation service.

Rabbi Cohen liked all the festivals of the year. They helped teach people of the close ties Judaism has to nature and what a blessing nature can be to us. They also were a reminder of how much Judaism is a part of the daily lives of the Jews.

Upon his arrival at the dean's office, Rabbi Cohen shared some of his funny stories about the medical school, and they had a mutual laugh. At lunch, Dr. Cohen again told the dean that there were monies available if he knew of students who couldn't afford to attend school. Afterwards, Cohen left for his library at home. He wanted to be there when it was time to speak with the governor at 3:00 P.M.

As Dr. Cohen's car moved down Seawall

Boulevard, his eye wandered to the Balinese Room. The wonderfully historical club and restaurant stretched out over the Gulf waters some several hundred yards and some twenty-plus feet above the water. He remembered when the very end of the structure was approximately the location of the home plate of one of the Island's baseball fields. The Island used to stretch some several hundred yards out into the Gulf of Mexico prior to the 1900 storm.

Rabbi Cohen could never forget the 1900 storm. This hurricane, labeled as the worst natural disaster to occur in the United States, killed 6,000 people including several members of Temple B'nai Israel.

It was on a Saturday morning in September that the storm began to affect the Island, and Cohen and his family rode out the storm in the home of a neighbor, Mr. Lee. Following the storm, the Rabbi made his way to the hospital to see if he could be of any help. The scene was one of total destruction — large holes in the land, trees turned over everywhere, huge piles of wood and debris that used to be homes and buildings. There were so many dead, it was impossible to bury them all, so the community planned to float them out on barges and bury them at sea. This did not work, as the tide washed the bodies back on shore. The bodies had to be piled up and burned.

As the community began to rebuild,

Rabbi Cohen was appointed, along with Mr. Kempner, to the committee for rebuilding the Island. In a 1902 letter, Clara Barton, one of the founders of the American Red Cross who came to help with the rebuilding of the Island, wrote of Cohen's great efforts, concluding with the words, "the gratitude of a heart never to be expressed to yourself." A year later, she corresponded with Cohen about teaching first aid around the country and sought his suggestions.

After the storm, the community literally raised the Island by jacking up all the buildings and pumping sand under each one. Also, a seawall was built on the Gulf side of the Island.

Passing the county jail, Dr. Cohen remembered that in Texas the use of a bull whip had been permitted on the naked backs of prisoners in state prisons. The whip was a leather strap, several inches wide, with a heavy knot at the end and attached to a wooden handle. Not only was the prison treatment harsh, but no system existed for those who were released from prison following the completion of their sentence. Beatings in Texas were not limited to adults, but children received them as well.

On one occasion, the only thing which stood between a teenager and such treatment was the will of the Rabbi. Finding a judge unwilling to give a certain boy detention, Dr. Cohen locked himself, with the judge, in the judge's chambers, telling him that he would not open the door until the judge had given the boy parole. When the judge protested, Henry reminded him that before the judge changed his behavior, they had picked him out of many gutters while he was a confirmed drunk. The boy was released in the Rabbi's charge.

Not many people in Texas were in support of prison reform. Most thought that if a person was in prison, he didn't deserve much, and harsh treatment seemed acceptable. Rabbi Cohen did not agree. Cohen took every opportunity to speak on the issue, even in the train cars on which he was traveling. On one train trip a listener told the Rabbi that no Jew was going to tell Texans how to run their prisons. The Rabbi's traveling companion, John Darrouzet, a lawyer known as "the Black Eagle of the Gulf," had a private talk with the individual and converted him to a Cohen supporter.

Prison reform rested in the hands of the Legislature of Texas and the governor. At one point during the term of Governor Miriam Ferguson, the Legislature passed a prison reform bill. The governor vetoed it, however, as she said it would cost the state too much money. During the term of Governor Dan Moody, a prison reform bill passed, which included an eight-person board. Rabbi Cohen was appointed a member of that board.

It was to review these prison reforms that Rabbi Cohen planned to call Governor Coke Stevenson on this day in 1945. Even though it was some thirty years after the first reforms, Dr. Cohen knew that there were still many more goals that needed to be achieved. Prisoners were still not being helped to change their ways while in jail, and many returned on new sentences after finishing old ones. The Rabbi saw this as a waste of human beings and an incredible drain on state money.

That evening, following his afternoon phone visit with the governor, and after a quick dinner and a long day, the Rabbi took time to visit down the street in the dining room of one of his congregants. Over several drinks, two old friends reflected on many years on the Island and the many events in their lives. It was not an unusual event in the Rabbi's day, as his first task was that of pastor to his congregation. When asked why he had stayed so long on the Island, Dr. Cohen once commented that he had found good soil here and there was no reason to move.

5/Tidbits and a Legacy

As this tenth day of December drew to a close, Henry Cohen sat back in his library. He began thinking about a full day and a very satisfying life. Jewish tradition says we live on after our death in the memories that others have of us. The Rabbi knew he had produced many memories and a rich legacy.

Perhaps the greatest legacy that Rabbi Cohen left was the acting out of an early Jewish folktale. The folktale teaches that the world began with one person in order to show that helping one person is like helping everyone in the world. Rabbi Cohen's belief in this drove him to be involved with causes and people in need, no matter who they were. He was guided only by the words of the Prophet

Micah, "to do justly, to love mercy and to walk humbly with your God."

In addition to this legacy, another of Dr. Cohen's gifts to future generations would be the many stories told about him and the many different events that happened in his life. His long life is not the only reason for the many stories, but also his willingness to be involved with so many different people and causes.

The daily paper on this Monday, December 10, 1945, told of a very different world and city from the one more than fifty years earlier. Back in 1895, the most important events of the day were the dedication of the new statue of the Sacred Heart at Sacred Heart Church, a public discussion on the best use of the deepwater port that Galveston offered, and the arrival of the British steamship *Wilderspool*. Fifty years later, in 1945, the paper reported on the terrible events after World War II, including the destruction of European Jews, and other events such as Gen. Douglas MacArthur establishing farming reforms in conquered Japan, and Gen. George Patton having just been seriously injured in an automobile accident in Mannheim, Germany. Henry Cohen was a part of both times and involved with people in each period.

To have a better understanding of Dr. Cohen's involvement with people, all one has to do is look at his correspondence. It is amazing that from 1907 to 1908 alone, he received over 2,000 letters — from family, friends, children of friends, ex-students, people he helped, societies, leagues, governors of Texas, the U.S. State Department, congregations looking for rabbis, congregations looking to dismiss rabbis, mental patients' families, prisoners, prisoners' families, Mexican Jews, the UAHC, HUC, orphanages, cities, marriages, and people with theological questions.

In 1925, thinking about Judaism and his life, Rabbi Cohen wrote Harris L. Kempner: "Judaism is the most rational and reasonable form of faith in the world of today, and it contains elements that could make it the universal religion, if there is ever to be one. Every virtue of which the world boasts today is of Judaic thought, and even those fine ideas of lovingkindness and that find expression in Christianity and Muhammadanism, borrowed from Judaism though they be, are not followed by their exponents; hence, the religious prejudice of these days."

Rabbi Cohen's correspondence was only one part of his life and legacy. In 1914 he was elected to the first Board of Overseers of the Hebrew Union College, the Rabbinical school of the Reform movement. Over the years, he was an ardent supporter of the college. His grandson, Henry, attended the Cincinnati campus. In 1948 Cohen sent a letter to HUC saying that his grandson would be conducting services in Galveston and therefore would be eligible for a 50% clergy pass book for the railroad. His letter not only helped Henry the student, but Henry the Rabbi as well, as it provided him with an assistant for the holy days.

Not everything that Dr. Cohen did was of a serious nature. In 1896 he won a contest to name a hall in New Orleans. It was to be called the Athenaeum. The Rabbi won $25 — not much today, but clearly a good amount in those days.

Cohen didn't worry much about his income. He didn't even always keep money he was given for his work. One person who sent Cohen expense money, which the Rabbi returned, said that was nothing more than Cohen's usual style.

In 1903 Rabbi Cohen received a letter from the chief of police concerning gambling in Galveston. In the correspondence, he mentioned several members of the congregation and the amount of gambling they did. He hoped that Cohen would do something about it, and he did. Though the Rabbi could not stop people from participating, at least they knew that he was watching.

Clearly, Rabbi Cohen felt very comfortable involving himself in the lives of those for whom he cared. For many years, Cohen had been in contact with the Jewish community in Mexico. He was especially concerned that they grew and prospered. In 1908 he even arranged for Rabbi G. Deutsch to conduct services in Mexico City for the Jewish community there.

In 1934 Cohen faced the worst for any parent. His daughter, Ruth, was diagnosed with Hodgkin's disease, for which little treatment was available in those days. She died that year, and the Rabbi insisted upon officiating at her funeral in their home. Cohen's words are still remembered by many who were there. With his trembling hand on her coffin, the distraught father recited the words from the Book of Job in the Bible, "though He slay me, yet shall I put my trust in Him." To the community, his words have remained as an overwhelming example of faith.

When Henry was new to Galveston, there were no public libraries. As a result, he began to create his own library by ordering books, both from the United States and from Europe. It was the only way that Dr. Cohen could continue his studies. When he retired, more than 2,000 volumes were given to the University of Texas Library in Austin. Dr. Cohen thought more students might make use of his library at the University of Texas than in Galveston.

Unfortunately, the Rabbi lived to see the destruction of most of the Jews in Europe by the Nazis. Moreover, he saw the silence of the Christian population in the United States, people of otherwise good will, who never hesitated to call upon him for help. The Rabbi was terribly sad over this horrible silence.

The stories of Dr. Cohen always involved the needs of others and always demonstrated his willingness to work with anyone. He always strove to reach for the highest in achievement and encouraged others to do the same thing. He was privileged to experience a congregation which supported him in all his activities. They learned from him, and they drew great pleasure and pride from all that he did.

Rabbi Henry Cohen's greatest legacy was his ability to bring to life the teachings of the Bible and Judaism. He conveyed those teachings to everyone with whom he came into contact. Dr. Cohen believed that the obligation of Jews was to act in a way that showed the world the best people could achieve. He spent his life trying to achieve this goal, even up to the day of his death, June 12, 1952.

There was a young man with little or no means who wished to enter the Episcopal ministry. He had a problem because he had no way to learn the subject of Christology. He came to ask Rabbi Cohen for help. Without hesitating, Cohen offered to teach the young man just as he had learned it in London. The Episcopal seminary was surprised when the young man was asked where he studied Christianity. The answer was "under Rabbi Henry Cohen." The student was admitted and given credit for the work.

The idea of the Jewish people being chosen simply meant that they had an obligation to teach and behave according to the words of Scripture and Jewish tradition. They were to be a light to the rest of the world. Cohen wrote that "the Jews are no better or no worse than their fellow citizens of other denominations. They are not white; they aren't black, but gray, like everybody else. In a country that gives them equal opportunity they rise to the general level and sometimes surpass it. They give more than their share of blood in time of war and their equal share of wealth and service in times of peace, as witness in your own state and your own community."

On the pulpit of Rabbi Cohen's congregation, B'nai Israel, are the words of his favorite quote from the book of Micah: "it has been told you, O man, what the Lord requires, to do justly, to love mercy and to walk humbly with your God." Dr. Cohen followed these words all his life. As a result, several generations were blessed by his presence — and all are blessed by the legacy he left behind.

Rabbi Henry Cohen, circa 1907.
—Courtesy Temple B'Nai Israel, Galveston

Mollie and Henry Cohen with their children, Ruth and Henry, 1899.

—Courtesy Temple B'Nai Israel, Galveston

Rabbi and Mrs. Henry Cohen, 1938.
—Courtesy Temple B'Nai Israel, Galveston

Confirmation Class of 1909. Row 1: Gladys Cohen, Esther Bonart; Row 2: Theresa Wansker, Leopold Wolters; Row 3: George Moskowitz, Esther Hauser, Clarence Milheiser, Selma Wansker, Harry Cohen, Ruth Schornstein.

—Courtesy Temple B'Nai Israel, Galveston

Confirmation class of 1931. Row 1: Jake Smith, Max Leaman; Row 2: Bertha Levy, Pearl Handler; Pauline Phillips, Lassie Posnick, Clara Baum, Fannie Helen Melcer; Row 3: Abe Levy, Sam Nussenblatt, Sara Kerson, J. N. Heidenheimer, Edna Mae Winter, Alfred Tocker, Henrietta Block, Bernard Tinterow.

—Courtesy Temple B'Nai Israel, Galveston

The Rabbi and the Temple he served for more than half a century, Temple B'Nai Israel, Galveston.
—Courtesy Temple B'Nai Israel, Galveston

Mayor Herbert Cartwright, Rabbi Cohen, Rabbi Louis Feigon, captain of Israeli ship, 1948.

—Courtesy Temple B'Nai Israel, Galveston

The Rabbi in his later years.
—Courtesy Temple B'Nai Israel, Galveston

Glossary

American Mission to the Jews — a group of people who try to convert Jews to Christianity because they believe Judaism is not a good religion.

anti-Semitism — hostility toward or disccrimination against Jews as a religious or racial group or individuals.

B.C.E. — before the common era; beginning of the numbering of years otherwise referred to as B.C., before Christ.

Bible — in Jewish tradition, the term "Bible" refers to the Hebrew Scriptures. These books are often referred to as the Old Testament in Christian tradition.

CCAR — Central Conference of American Rabbis; the professional rabbinical organization of Reform Rabbis.

Chanukah — the name means "dedication" and refers to the festival which commemorates the Maccabees' victory over the Syrians around 150 B.C.E. The Jews were able to drive the Syrians out of the Temple in Jerusalem, remove the idols placed in it, and return to the worship of God.

chanukiyah — in addition to the military battle commemorated by Chanukah, there is a story told of the miracle of the eight days. The eternal light, which was always kept burning in the Temple and which today is why a light is always kept burning in churches and synagogues, was put out by the Syrians. Once the Jews took over the Temple and wanted to rekindle the light, they found they had oil for only one day; however, the oil burned for eight days until more could be made. The miracle was that the light lasted for all those eight days. To remember those days, a candelabra called a **chanukiyah** which contains eight candles plus one to light them is used to observe the festival.

chauffeur — an individual who is paid to drive an owner around in the owner's car.

circumcision — surgical removal of the foreskin from a male's penis; when done according to the Jewish tradition, it takes place on the eighth day of the child's life.

confirmation — a ritual ceremony usually observed at the age of fifteen which notes the completion of one segment of Jewish education.

czar — term for a Russian king.

deport — to send a person who has entered a country illegally back to their home country.

Exodus — refers to the Children of Israel, the Jews, leaving the land of Egypt for the promised land; the event is usually dated around 1300 B.C.E.

frock coat — a style of coat worn by gentlemen at the turn of the twentieth century.

Galveston Plan — a program which was run from 1907 to 1914, and was designed to help settle new immigrants from Europe who came through the port of Galveston.

Gilbert and Sullivan — two famous British composers from the nineteenth century; created such works as *The Pirates of Penzance.*

Hasmoneans — another name for the Jews who fought against the Syrians and from which Chanukah arose; another name for them was the Maccabees.

Hebrew — the language of the Jewish people; the original language of the Bible. Today it is the language spoken in modern Israel and is used as a language of prayer outside of Israel.

Hodgkin's Disease — a form of cancer which used to result in death and today can be cured.

Holocaust — the term refers to the destruction of European Jewry by the Nazis; the only known example in human history where the humanity of the slain was taken away from them. Dead of war and other battles are usually left for their families or friends, while the Nazis used every part of the Jews to profit the Nazi government — skin for lamp shades, hair for pillows, etc.

honorary doctorate degrees — some colleges and universities honor special individuals by giving them an honorary doctor's degree, which is not acquired academically.

HUC — Hebrew Union College; the Reform Rabbinical School established in Cincinnati, Ohio, in 1875; later merged with the Jewish Institute of Religion in New York.

Jew's Hospital — a very old institution in London which provided hospital care for poor folk and ran schools for poor children.

Kaffir — a member of a group of South African Bantu-speaking people.

Ku Klux Klan — a secret society started at the end of the Civil War demanding white supremacy; organized to keep free slaves from obtaining civil rights. Today their targets are Jews, African Americans, and Catholics.

latkes — eastern European traditional food eaten at Chanukah time; similar to potato pancakes.

legacy — something left by an ancestor in the past; can refer to the way an ancestor lived his or her life and the way others would want to copy it in the future.

malady — an illness or something that has ill effects.

matzah — unleaven bread eaten during the festival of Passover.

mohel — a member of the Jewish community trained to perform ritual circumcisions for Jewish males on the eighth day of their lives.

Monsignor — a Roman Catholic priest who receives this title as an honor from the Pope.

Montifiore, Lord Moses — one of the most prominent British Jews in the 1800s; a major contributor to numerous charities in England, both Jewish and non-Jewish.

Passover — the festival observed in the spring celebrating the exodus of the Jews from Egypt so that they might worship God as they wanted; one of the three pilgrimage festivals commanded in the Bible.

Pharaoh — the title for the ruler of ancient Egypt.

pilgrimage — a journey taken to sacred places; another way of describing a course of life on earth.

pogroms — an organized massacre of helpless people, usually referring to the destruction of Jews in Europe.

Prophets — the second major part of the Bible; refers to those who uttered divinely inspired revelations in biblical days.

rabbinage — the unique name given to the home owned by Temple B'nai Israel and used by the Rabbis of the congregation.

Reform Judaism — a branch of the modern Jewish community organized in the United States in the middle of the 1800s; today the largest group of Jews in the United States.

schochet — title given to an individual trained to slaughter appropriate food animals according to Jewish law.

seder — the ritual evening meal eaten in celebration of the festival of Passover.

Shabbat — the most important day observed in Jewish tradition; established in the creation story as a day of rest applying to every person and all animals.

Shavuot — festival of "weeks" which commemorates the giving of the Torah on Mount Sinai by God to Moses; one of the three major pilgrimage festivals commanded in the Bible.

stowaway — one who secrets himself aboard a vehicle in order to get transportation.

Sukkot — the festival of "booths" where the Jews traveled to Jerusalem to observe the festival in the Temple; the booths made of palm leaves and wood today represent the booths which were used for dwelling 2,000 years ago.

synagogue — a Jewish house of worship; other words for such a house are **temple** and **shul.**

temple — the Jewish house of worship built by King Solomon to the glory of God in about 970 B.C.E.; after it was destroyed in 586 B.C.E., it was rebuilt and used until it was destroyed in 70 C.E.

Torah — the first five books of the Bible, also called the **Pentateuch.** The Bible records that this was what Moses was given by God on Mount Sinai.

traitor — a person who gives away harmful information concerning his country to someone else.

UAHC — Union of American Hebrew Congregations; the organization of Reform synagogues in the United States and Canada.

Yom Kippur — the day of atonement observance during which Jews fast and spend the day in prayer and reflection; next to the Sabbath it is considered the most sacred day in the ritual Jewish year.

Zulu — a member of the Bantu-speaking people in Natal, South Africa.

Bibliography

Books:

Cohen, Harry, and Anne Nathan. *The Man Who Stayed in Texas.* McGraw Hill, 1941.

Dreyfus, A. Stanley. *Henry Cohen: Messenger of the Lord.* Bloch Publishing, 1963.

Hyman, Harold. *Oleander Odyssey.* College Station: Texas A&M Press, 1990.

Kessler, Jimmy. *B.O.I., A History of Congregation B'Nai Israel, Galveston, Texas.* Unpublished doctoral dissertation, 1988.

Levy, Adrian. *I Love Life.* Privately published and distributed.

Miller, Ray. *Galveston.* Houston: Gulf Publishing, 1983.

New Handbook of Texas. Austin: Texas State Historical Association, 1996.

Winegarten, Ruthe, and Cathy Schechter. *Deep in the Heart.* Austin: Eakin Press, 1990.

Interviews:

The author was privileged to interview many individuals who have since died. All were lifelong residents of Galveston, Texas, and many were members of Congregation B'nai Israel. Among those interviewed in this group were Ms. Mathilde Colby, Mrs. Eleanor Bodansky, Mr. and Mrs. Adrian Levy, Sr., Mr.

Adam Levy; Mrs. Edna Levin, Mrs. Evelyn Krantz, Mr. Lewis Harris, Father Charles Anasthasia, Mr. and Mrs. Joseph Levy, Mr. C.Q. Ammons, Ms. Nettie Schornstein, Mr. Ray Schornstein, Mrs. Ethel Nierman, Mrs. Pearl Stein, Mr. Alphonse Hamilton, Mrs. Iwin M. Herz, Mr. Bob Nesbit, Mr. Harris L. Kempner, Dr. Abe Levy, and Mrs. Jeanette Lipson. In addition, the author is very grateful to Rabbi Cohen's daughter-in-law, Annie, his grandson Henry, and his colleague Stanley Dreyfus, who have extended me every kindness in preparing this work and who have done much to preserve Dr. Cohen's heritage.

A great deal of thanks is due to the members of Congregation B'nai Israel who have kept the memory of Rabbi Henry Cohen alive. Their telling of stories about him has insured that people who come after them would appreciate his legacy. The author wishes to thank all of those who cared enough to share their experiences. In addition, special thanks to Peggy Boening for her time and assistance in organizing this manuscript. To my children, Andy Joshua and Jenny Ann, and to my wife and partner, Shelley Gail, my love and gratitude for allowing me to compose this work.